Kramer the Gamer

First Published by

Text copyright @ Margaret McArthur
Illustrations copyright @ Margaret McArthur

All rights reserved. No part of this publication may be used or reproduced, stored or introduced into a retrieval system, or transmitted, in any form or by any means (electronic, mechanical, photocopying, recording or otherwise), without the prior written permission of the publisher - except in case of brief quotations used in reviews and/or academic articles, in which case quotations are permitted.

Written by Margaret McArthur
Illustrated by Bryan Jason Ynion (BJY)
Layout by Carolyn Tonkin Design
Printed by Ingramspark

National Library of Australia
Cataloguing-in-Publication data:
Margaret McArthur 2019

ISBN
978-0-6484449-4-7 (Paperback)
978-0-6484449-5-4 (Hardback)

For children age 6-10
Subjects covered, game addiction, online presence, technology use.

First Edition

This publication contains ideas and opinions of the author and is a fictional story. It is intended as a resource for informing children on the dangers of game addiction. Educators are advised to read through the book before commencing delivery to the intended audience.

The author and publisher assume no responsibility for any liability, loss or risk, personal or otherwise, which is incurred consequently, directly or indirectly, of the use and application of any content of this book.

This book is dedicated to my son Bailey,
your smile brings joy to my heart.

Kramer was a young Robot, who loved to play computer games. His friends joined him online, they all used their nicknames. The bots ran, kicked and jumped through the levels. Kramer always won the challenges and with it, the medals.

He was **exceptionally** skilled in this online space.
His car won him top scores in the **virtual** race.

His friends tried to beat him, but they couldn't compete.
Kramer was that good, they admitted **Defeat.**

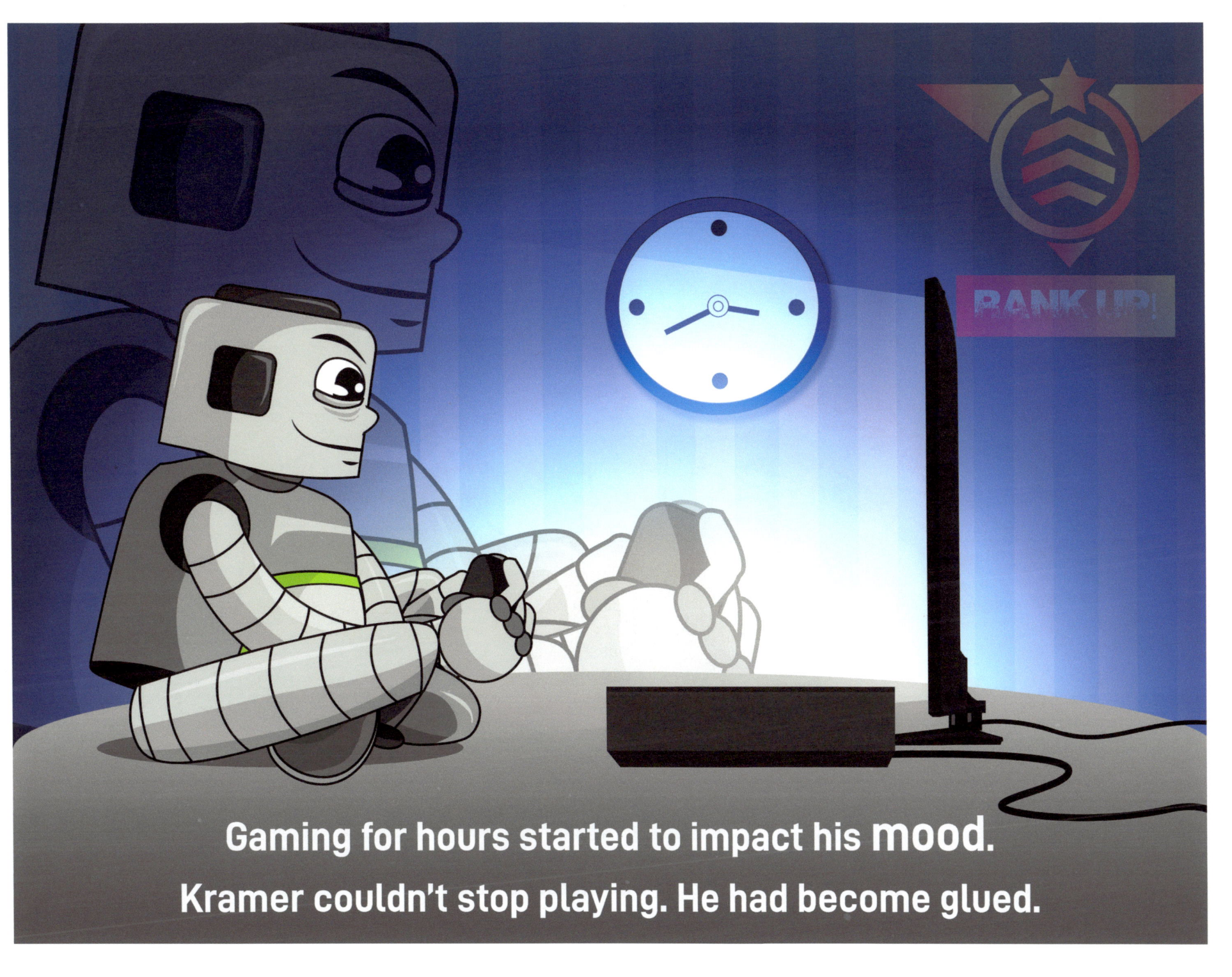

When the morning came, Kramer couldn't get out of bed.

He told his mother he was tired and had a sore head.

The games were intense, he would play for hours.
He stopped brushing his teeth and wouldn't take showers!

His parents were **concerned** about the impact of the game.
They worried that the **violence** would influence his brain.

They discussed with Kramer about ending this game addiction.
His time online was excessive and needed some restriction.

Kramer **bitterly** agreed, but said nothing for days.
Still addicted to playing, **sneaking** online other ways.
He installed new apps on his mobile phone
and played **his** games whenever he was alone.

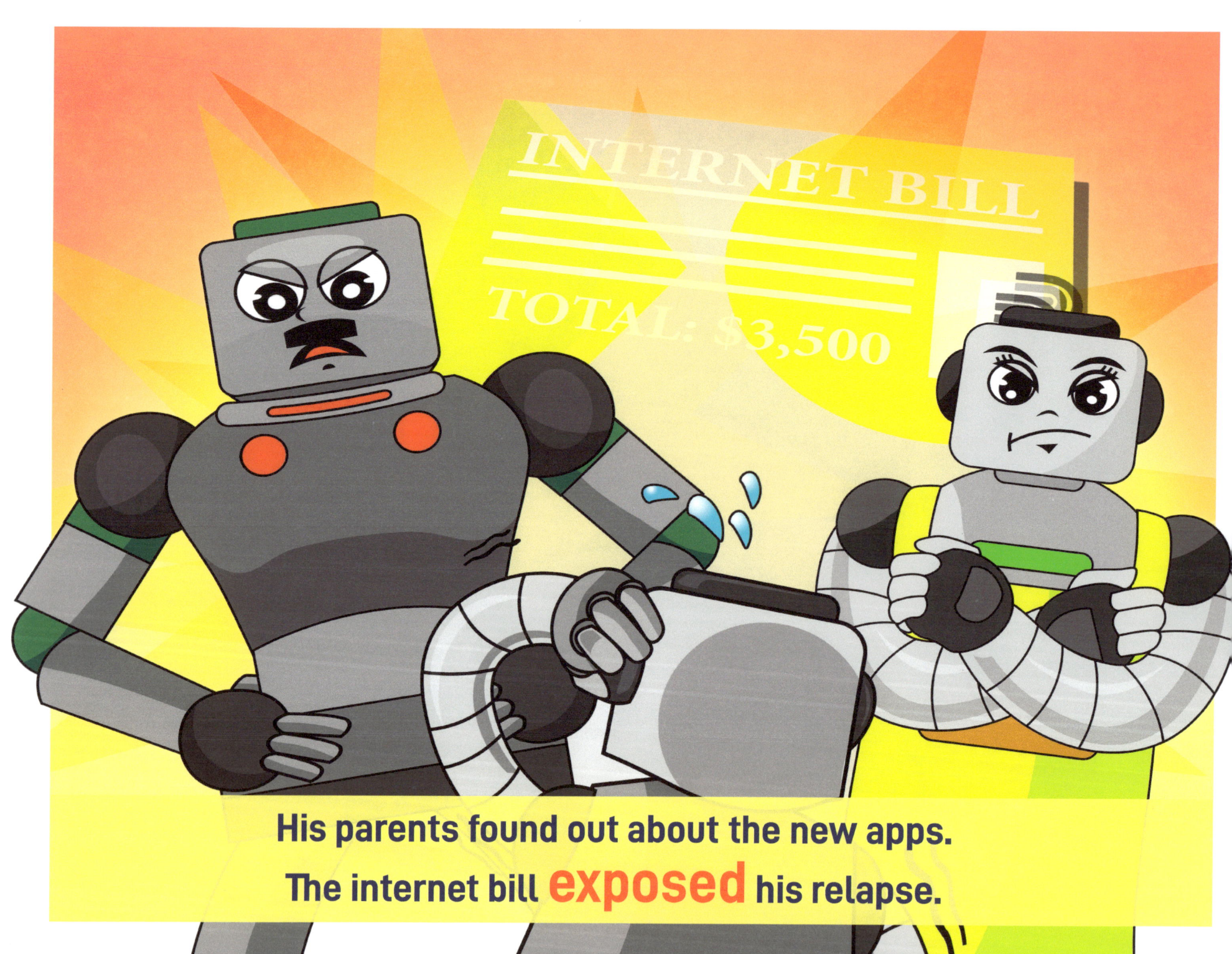

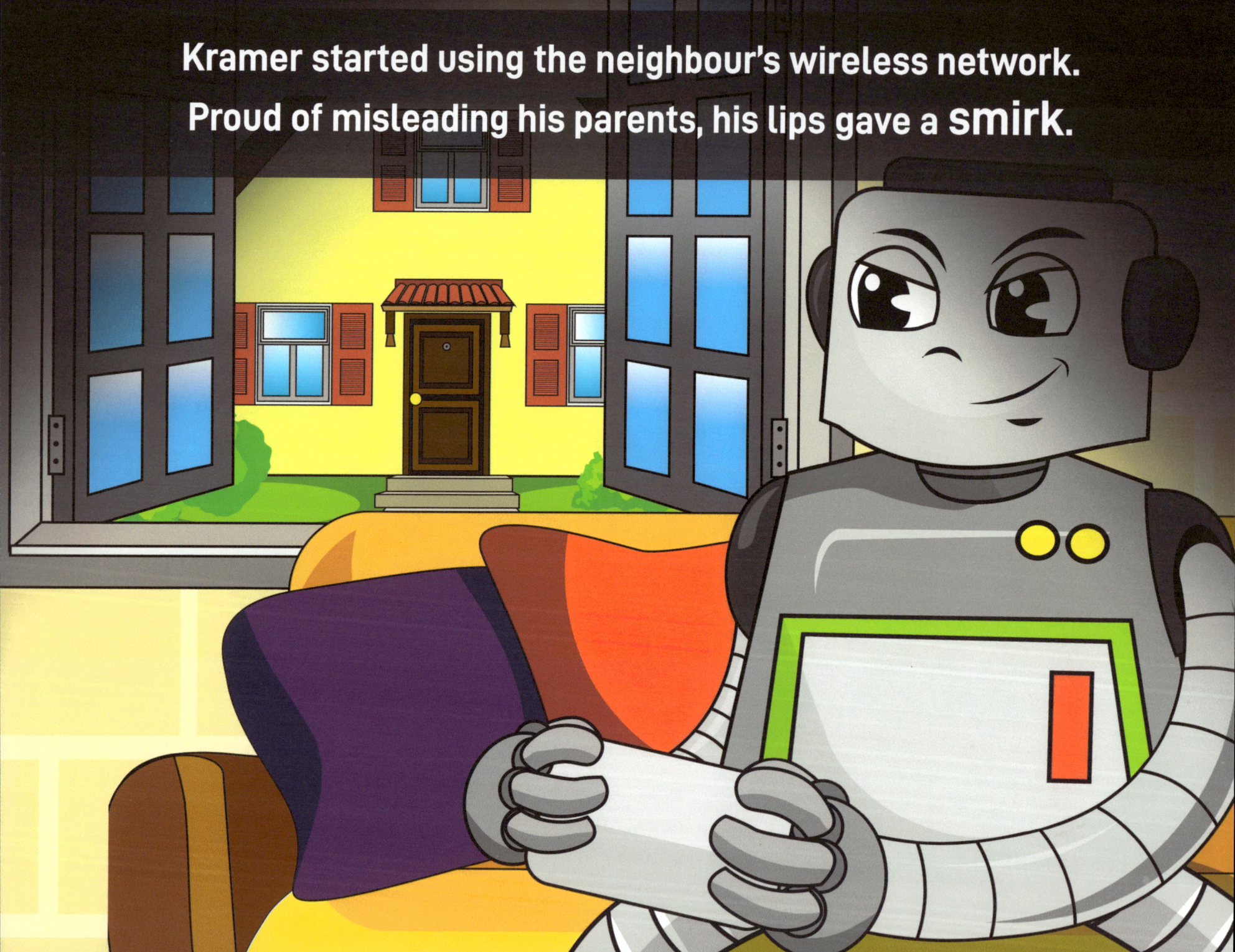

The neighbour's discovered what he had done.
Kramer's dad was furious with the actions of his son.

He tried to deny using the neighbour's internet.
But the invoice revealed Kramer's large debt.

**Kramer began to sob, confessing all he had done.
His road to recovery had finally begun.**

He struggled to ignore his device at night.
Refraining from playing took all of his might.

Kramer felt guilty for keeping this quiet.
If he was discovered, there would be a riot.
He found it difficult to stick to the plan.
So he set small targets and enforced a self-ban.

He began to play sport with his friends outside.
This transformation filled the family with pride.

Kramer enjoyed playing soccer and netball.
He loved hockey and cricket, anything with a ball.

His friendships deepend and became even stronger.
Outside at the park, he stayed longer and longer.

His attention in class had also improved.

Displaying enthusiasm, the teacher approved.

His online **addiction** over time did lessen.
Kramer had learned a valuable life-lesson.

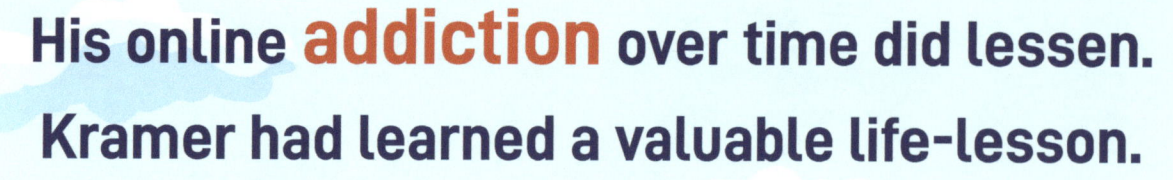

He became happy and content with his **active** lifestyle.
Playing sport with his friends gave him the biggest smile.

Kramer still plays in the Virtual Race,

but times and supervision were put into place.

He and his parents now laugh and chat all the time.

They enjoy playing games, especially the

mime!

Margaret McArthur is a teacher and leader of technology in Victoria. Since starting her teaching career in Scotland over a decade ago as a Secondary Computing teacher, she discovered a passion for eLearning, which encompassed the implementation and overview of the school Cyber Awareness program. The evolution of the program required early intervention of education in the younger year levels, due to the increased use of technology at an early age. With this increase of time online, children are more exposed to the pitfalls of the internet.

With education and support, our children can learn how to make informed decisions online as they learn to keep themselves safe in the real world. This led to the creation of her cyber safe books, addressing various aspects of online dangers to protect our children from external threats.

www.margaretmcarthur.com.au

www.ingramcontent.com/pod-product-compliance
Lightning Source LLC
Chambersburg PA
CBHW041326290426

44110CB00004B/150